www.cagliastrotheironring.com

www.northseatales.com

Advanced Class Transcript Books, a new series by
North Sea Tales Inc. featuring transcripts of SEDATIONS and
ADVANCED CLASSES in the techniques of
The Science of Sorcery.

SELF EFFIGY

AND THE USE OF

EFFIGY ON OTHERS

Two Expanded Sedation transcripts (live presented with
Instillations, recordings available) discussing the use of Paper
and Clay Effigies as applied to the Self and as applied to Others
with Core Insertions and a thorough explanation of the use of
Biologicals, Thoughts, Ideas, Intentions, Directional Sorcery
and Polarities , Require and Desire, Outcome Manipulation –
and of course.....the attainment of
PLEASURE
By SORCERESS CAGLIASTRO
Copyright 2018
PRODUCED BY NORTH SEA TALES PUBLISHING INC.

This is a set of Sedation (One Time Only classes) transcripts. There are lightly edited and profoundly enhanced for clarity. These transcripts are in the language and speaking style of The Sorceress. This transcript is enhanced with additional material and comments by Sorceress Cagliastro.

THE SIGIL FOR "KNOWING"

This book is a product of
NORTH SEA TALES PUBLISHING INC.
www.northseatales.com

GENERAL INTRODUCTION AS APPLIES TO <u>BOTH PARTS</u> OF THIS BOOK

Why do I call these SEDATIONS? Well the answer is two-fold. First, it is because I am utilizing the Science of Sorcery which lives within the process of understanding that thoughts Ideas and Intention have weight. We are not doing mystical work handed over by some "deity" here tonight – or ever in my work. We are in fact learning a method of manipulation that is 100% valid, tested, proven, replicate-able, if that's a word, and supported by the data of success. The second reason is that I teach the work inside of the Collective Consciousness of all of this data, and therefore there is an opportunity to imbed the process into your skill set.

This is an enriched transcript. It is not a novel.
It is written accordingly.
(Think "cookbook" not "storybook")

The RECORDINGS of these 2 SEDATIONS are available for rent here:

https://www.cagliastrotheironring.com/recordings-library.html

NOTE:
Parameter of Intention for the Self Effigy is defined as the selected use and method of Effigies.

DIRECTIONAL SORCERY (applies to both sections of this book)

I am adding these notes regarding DIRECTIONAL SORCERY – even for those of you who have no exposure to it. As the polarities avail themselves of additional energies that are proactive. If you are already familiar with Directional Sorcery – then enjoy the ride. If you are not – then you are receiving a bonus here that can be utilized in other aspects of Sorcery as well.

Now we review the Polarities.

The polarities are earth/magnetic points that influence the outcome of the work. They are in NO WAY mystical, associated with divinities or angles or watchtowers or whatever other dogma you have carried. They are quite simply members of the laws of physics. For the many decades I have been doing this work, I can assure you that the data has PROVEN that these are the categories of assistance provided by the polarities:

SOUTHERN WORK – REMOVAL

NORTHERN WORK – INSERTION OF SKILLS

WESTERN WORK – RESUSCITATION of previous or lost skills reinserted at a digestible pace. It can also be acted upon by **DROWING** and resuscitation of the Effigy.

EASTERN WORK – to accelerate your expectations. I hate the term MANAGE your expectation. This is Sorcery – all you have to manage is how much PLEASURE you feel you can take in and at what speed. Hint – the answer is 'all of it and right now'.....

When we work with polarities – for example when I say "place it in the NORTH" – I am saying the NORTH as it applies from where you stand. Where you stand is, for the purpose of Directional Sorcery, the CENTER of the compass. Therefore I refer in my work to the center-point as the **"HUMAN COMPASS"**.

Place the head of the SELF EFFIGY into the polarity that best suits your purpose. By this I am saying you should place the Effigy not only in that polarity – for greater efficiency, place it's head also facing into the polarity. Place it down with purpose. Slam it of place it gently – whichever best suits your intention. You are alone and have all rights to do this as you please.

THE BIOLOGICALS
Applies to both parts of this book

Biologicals are the address on the envelope. Remember that. This isn't mystical. When we use or DNA we are saying that THIS OBJECT is an extension of ourselves and that we are the actual one performing the task. If your core DNA is in an effigy doll to be used on someone else, then you are already under their skin because you are already inside of them. The synapse is real – there are chemicals and electricity to support it – and now you are in there – already doing the work. So therefore the type of biological we use is relevant as it goes to our willingness to put ourselves into the work. Here is a list from the strongest to the least powerful of the Biologicals.

1. Arterial Blood or VENAL Blood. Drawn by syringe
2. Harvested Blood
3. Sexual fluid
4. Hair with follicles
5. Nails and skin and saliva
6. Products of digestion etc....

This is the order of intensity, of course, there are situations where the choice is made from association to the circumstance:

If your intention or HISTORY regarding the EFFIGY is overtly sexual in nature, semen and other sexual fluids can of course be added to the core of the EFFIGY. REMEMBER AT ALL TIMES THAT THIS SEDATION IS ABOUT EFFIGIES on others – so YOUR biologicals must be in the core if you are using them.

Regarding the collection of YOUR biologicals – all the usual methods apply.

Prepare those materials – be prepared to harvest your Blood with a tiny scalpel or lancet, prepare Semen and other fluids via masturbation as this is SELF EFFIGY. All and all this manner of Sorcery puts you back in the driver's seat of your life. I say BACK intentionally, it allows for you to realize, in your hands – that it is all in your control.

When gathering the biologicals of the OTHER – do what you have to do without getting caught. If you do not have their biologicals, then you will add something to the work to represent them. Something they have touched is also useful.

-PART ONE-
SELF EFFIGY

PRINCIPLES, USE, CONSTRUCTION AND PROCESS SPECIFIC TO UTILIZING EFFIGY ON THE SELF

This SEDATION occurred on 4/5/18

OPENING NOTES

THIS is a 90 or so minute Sedation during which the participants are exposed to the information regarding the use and construction of Self Effigies (Effigies for use on others is covered in PART TWO of this book). By the end of the Sedation, Students will be will be left with your Self Effigy and decide how to complete its process resulting in your desired experience. (In the live class students made the Self Effigy. Readers should read through the entire book before starting) I leave it that way on purpose so that you can hear the best result through communication with the Self Effigy and your requirement of release or attainment. As you are to use brown paper to make the Self Effigies, you will literally be left HOLDING THE BAG – in other words – fully involved with your decision.

Within that 90 or so minutes of time I will show you how most useful three methods of the making twisted paper SELF EFFIGIES through photos of the pieces. (NOTE - there is a difference between self effigies and effigies of others and their most useful manner of construction. Effigies for use on OTHERS is covered in PART TWO of this book.) I have taught many classes on the making of things, and I can tell you that there is nothing more boring than watching someone who already knows how to make something- make it while teaching. Therefore I chose to use photos. The photos will show up in the recording, and are also in this book (readers may rent the recordings as well) and therefore, as everyone in this class *(when it was live)* will get a 48 hour review of this sedation so that you can review the work – you can pace yourself and construct at a comfortable pace.

That being said, in the final half hour or so, (during the live event) you will be constructing a twisted paper self-effigy. No art critics are watching – so have no concerns at the level of your construction. Working in this Sedation tonight is your first, well for some of you – your first attempt at this work. As a teacher of these materials, I find it vital to support the students by offering the recording as I stated, and by answering email questions so that you can use your relaxed mind now to simply take in the work.

That being said – do take notes.

> That which is written in your own hand at the time of
> first hearing is
> always precious and may reveal
> data about the self as you write.

Also, I must remind students when making objects that are only devices in Sorcery (as most of the work happens in the mind) that the quest for greater skills is splendid – the quest for PERFECTION of these temporary devices is poisonous to the self...... Effigies must be "just enough" to complete the task....

SO on that note – listen carefully - It is important NOT to become attached to Effigies. They are meant to disintegrate, to become something either absorbed or discarded. Either way, aside from particular cases, they CANNOT remain intact or the process is not complete. These effigies are not DOLLS, they are not ART and they are not voodoo dolls. They cannot be, because this is not voodoo -all due respect to voodooists – that is just not my method. What we are doing here tonight is making edits and additions to THE SELF.

The structure of tonight's Sedation is this – I will utilize approximately a full hour explaining the ways in which the SELF EFFIGY works, categories etc., all manner of information arranged in an organized fashion as the human mind is satisfied by equation....

Remember, this is NOT a Sedation about working on others, apart from the moments where I discuss placing something of yourself into another. Those types of manipulations will be explored further in the second of these classes, **(PART TWO ON THIS BOOK)** (which occurred May 17/18)– if you choose to participate in that one.

TONIGHT I AM GOING TO COVER THE FOLLOWING CATEGORIES:

1. TWELVE CATEGORIES FOR SELF EFFIGY use as
   defined by nuances
2. METHODS OF CONSTRUCTION
3. RESOLUTIONS
   (what to do with them including Blood Sorcery)
4. RELATIONSHIP OF USES TO THE POLARITIES aka
DIRECTIONAL SORCERY

These instructions will overlap a bit – as that is the nature of process.

I choose to place this section BEFORE the SECTION THAT TELLS THE READER HOW TO MAKE THE EFFIGIES. I DO SO THAT YOU ARE FULLY INFORMED AS YOU GO THROUGH THE WORK.

You MUST read the ENTIRE BOOK before beginning the Effigy work in order to get the best results.

TWELVE CATEGORIES FOR SELF EFFIGY USE AS DEFINED BY NUANCES

1. TO REMOVE A DILEMMA OR HABIT. This is an interrupter. Habit is broken by causing one to not continue, or not finish what one has chosen to begin. This also helps one to escape the confusion (not the outcome) of decision making. More simply, use this to stop or remove habits. The effigy in this case represents the habit inside of the self.

   PLACED IN EFFIGY – for a habit that is causing behavioral issues but does not involve a chemical yet is causing an interruption of process, use semen or sexual fluids, and a hair with a follicle. Useful also for sex addiction. For **physical** habits such as addiction to drugs or alcohol, use Blood.

   TECHNIQUE – create the twisted paper effigy of your choice while stating its purpose. Add the biological/s into the paper that will be the body head for a behavior that is does not involve chemicals and in the body core for one that does. If you are not sure of the category, place the biologicals in the body core. SUGGESTED POLARITY – as we are breaking with a habit/addiction/ use SOUTH.

2. TO REMOVE OR RESTRUCTURE A PHYSICAL DIS-COMFORT, DIS-EASE, UN-WELLNESS. Use this when taking on more of the responsibility for healing or changing the body in some way.

   PLACED IN EFFIGY – BLOOD, arterial if possible

TECHNIQUE - create the twisted paper effigy of your choice. Add the biological/s into the paper that will be the body core. Continue adding it to the legs and the back of the head as well. SUGGESTED POLARITY – Place the effigy South West first, then after a full 24 hour period place it fully South.

3. TO REMOVE DOGMA. Use when intellectual blockages such as the data or dogma which supports guilt or emotional hangovers are in the way. Even use this when the individual has ALREADY MADE an INTELLECTUAL break with dogma, and there are residual drags. They can be removed via self-effigy work.
PLACED IN EFFIGY – hair with follicles, saliva and semen or menstrual Blood
TECHNIQUE- create the twisted paper effigy of your choice while stating its purpose. Place the biologicals in the HEAD - SUGGESTED POLARITY – Place South for 24 hours, South East for 24 Hours, then South again for 24 hours.

4. TO INCREASE INCOMING CAPABILITIES. This is used to increase the amount of "incoming" one can handle. The key word here is increase, to increase the amount one can learn, to increase the amount one can handle, to increase the amount one allows themselves to require or desire, to increase the amount of any incoming that represents a change in life structure moving away from dogma. Think of this as "THE PERMISSION

SLIP" – (which is going to be the focus of my teaching going forward in late 2018 – contact me for more information.)

PLACED IN EFFIGY – Harvested Blood from two or more locations. I suggest this because the double harvest creates a relationship with chaos. CHAOS is required when seeking "more". I would place the Blood on "pulse points" on the effigy (neck, wrists etc.) PRIOR to wrapping it with thread, the repeat on top of the thread.

TECHNIQUE - create the twisted paper effigy of your choice while stating its purpose. - SUGGESTED POLARITY - Place North for 24 hours, North East for 24 Hours, then EAST again for 24 hours.

5. TO PERFORM INSERTIONS – This is the process of creating an external version of the self which contains the required and desired aspects which the individual would prefer to have as a nuance of personality. These externally designed "nuances" are put into an effigy, and then inserted into the self. This circumvents development at the internal level (a perfect use of Sorcery) which is often overly burdened with history.

PLACED IN EFFIGY – CREATE A SECOND SMALL EFFIGY and use Blood on the small one.

TECHNIQUE – placing the small effigy inside of the paper that will be the upper torso, create the twisted paper effigy of your choice while stating its purpose. - SUGGESTED POLARITY – North for 24 hours, then

North-East. While in North East add additional Blood to the top of the head of the external effigy. Then place the effigy East for 24 hours.

6. HARD RESET – To make massive sweeping changes. This can be anything from a significant personal change to a full change of identity. It can include the external aspects (even a change of name or gender) OR it is a profound scraping away and rebuilding of the self for private development. Edits are part of the natural flow of this option.
PLACED IN EFFIGY – all possible biologicals.
TECHNIQUE - create the twisted paper effigy of your choice while stating its purpose. Place it face down anywhere you will see it regularly. I suggest your mattress. After you have come to see it as yourself – add additional sexual fluids to the front of the effigy. SUGGESTED POLARITY – South for a few moments until you feel the connection, then SLOWLY over an hour or so to the North. Leave it there for as long as your senses feel is require. Then move it EAST and leave it there again until your sense tell you otherwise. Finally, place it NORTH.

7. TRAUMA EVISCERATION - This is a good strategy to remove KNOWN and UNKNOWN trauma. Nuance is important – trauma that is KNOWN is not necessarily remembered with accuracy – and it does not matter if the details are known because the feelings and experiences are what matters. So in a way, as all trauma is recalled

through a filter of damage – ALL trauma is unknown. Trauma can be assigned to the Self Effigy and removed. PLACED IN EFFIGY – BLOOD and sexual fluids. In this case Menstrual Blood is also an option. TECHNIQUE - create the twisted paper effigy of your choice while stating its purpose. Place the biologicals inside the torso, head and at the undersides of the feet. SUGGESTED POLARITY – West for a few moments, then South. Walk away for a while....

8. INSERTION OF A NEW BEGINNING. This is the Self Effigy of a new timeline. The Self Effigy is created as that which is NOT ATTACHED to your timeline, yet has had the experiences in the timeline, but in no particular order. The effigy can re-enter a "fresh" timeline and maintain the memories. PLACED IN EFFIGY – Hair with follicles and any other biological that feels appropriate to you. You can also include something that marks a new beginning for you. Example, tearing off the corner of a page of a lease or deed and including it in the effigy. TECHNIQUE - Place biologicals into the core and create the twisted paper effigy of your choice while stating its purpose. - SUGGESTED POLARITY -NORTH!!

9. MEMORY EVISCERATION – Memories are complex because they are not accurate generally speaking. HOW we remember something is not necessarily HOW the event occurred. I would go as far as to say that this applies

to ALL memories. Removing a memory allows for the self to remove all the attached interpretations, conflicts and "baggage" that may have become attached to the memory over time.

PLACED IN EFFIGY – BLOOD and saliva.

TECHNIQUE – Place the biologicals into the head and create the twisted paper effigy of your choice while stating its purpose. - SUGGESTED POLARITY – SOUTH.

10. TO REGAIN A SKILL OR MOMENT – To resuscitate that which has been suppressed or destroyed, refresh it by placing it in a new address in the timeline and re-energize the entire process of developing the skill.

PLACED IN EFFIGY – Blood from the chest area has proven the most effective for this category. Remember to make minimal and tiny incisions. You can also include something that triggers you regarding the skill of moment. A piece of a photo, an appointment card edge, an example of the skill (math equation, dance step image, degree letters etc.)

TECHNIQUE - create the twisted paper effigy of your choice while stating its purpose. - SUGGESTED POLARITY – Start West, turn slowly (going clockwise) to the East. Leave it there for 24 hours. Turn it NORTH.

11. TO PLACE YOURSELF INSIDE OF ANOTHER'S CONSCIOUSNESS – A living inhabitation is useful when one is working toward something that requires another person to fully engage. This is, in a way, similar to a living possession – HOWEVER it is not a control action. This technique gives the Practitioner an opportunity to be relevant and noticed throughout any process.

PLACED IN EFFIGY – create a tiny paper ball. Soak it in saliva. Name it.

TECHNIQUE - create the twisted paper effigy of your choice while stating its purpose. When wrapping it in thread, place the saliva ball on the forehead of the effigy. Wrap it against the effigy with the thread. SUGGESTED POLARITY – Place it East. Then move it counter clockwise to the WEST. Leave it there until you see yourself as though about by the target person. Then remove the paper ball and wrap it with thread to the back of the head. Place the effigy face down in the NORTH and leave it there.

12. TO PLACE ANOTHER'S SKILLS INSIDE OF YOU – Growing the capability through mimicry. When Sorcerers enact mimicry, they do not TAKE anything from the original source. One sees a circumstance that is attractive, and one mimics the NUANCE of the circumstance to use as a seed energy in another undertaking. For example, if someone wins a competition, the practitioner of Sorcery may mimic the

WIN, and utilize the energy and nuance of *that* win to win something else unrelated to the original contest.

PLACED IN EFFIGY – make a tiny effigy and mark it with something that represents the skill.

TECHNIQUE – place the tiny effigy in the torso while creating the twisted paper effigy of your choice while stating its purpose. Then put a drop of your BLOOD on the "eyes" of your self effigy.- SUGGESTED POLARITY - NORTH

METHODS and RESOLUTIONS

1. **CREATION OF THE EFFIGY** These Effigies are best made from twisted paper. The twisting is vital and the thread binds the twists. Allow me to expand on that statement. You will see that once you are creating these types of SELF EFFIGIES that techniques which support the forcing of YOURSELF into the SELF EFFIGY is a huge portion of the preparation. These are not paper dolls. The twisting provides 2 required insertions which connect the self to the object.

First, when twisting the paper you introduce your strength and by transference from your skin, your DNA into the piece. Your hands manipulate the paper and by the action of the twisting, you burn your own heat into it while doing so. The more paper Effigies you make, the more you will understand that the twisting is vital – it is visceral, even sensual in a way – it is pure physical transference.

Secondly the twisting brings the mind to the process as it has **sensation and occurs over time.** The twisting is CREATING. By contrast, if you were just cutting out a paper doll, or using a doll or object which already exists, then you would never ENGAGE in quite the same way. The physical Engagement is vital as it connects not only your physical self, but your mental self. Thoughts, Ideas and Intentions have weight. I have been saying this for years – lately some physicists and those studying neuroplasticity have caught on. *Good job.* As you twist the paper, you are drawn into the process. Distractions cannot beat out twisting when you are fully engaged in the process. Sounds around you become less relevant, thoughts outside of the process literally AT HAND fade away. This isn't paper anymore – this is a visceral connection – you are reaching in and touching your moment of change.

++

2. TREATMENT AND RESOLUTION OF THE EFFIGY

SELF EFFIGIES should be recipients of your DNA. I suggest BLOOD. If your intention for your SELF EFFIGY is overly sexual in nature, semen and other sexual fluids can of course be added to the SELF EFFIGY. REMEMBER AT ALL TIMES THAT THIS SEDATION IS ABOUT SELF EFFIGIES so the moving piece is YOU. I make suggestions in the 12 categories, however if a biological OTHER THAN the one I suggested, or if an ADDITIONAL biological feels right – make those adjustments.

Even when attracting something TO YOU – the POWER of this very different approach is that the moving piece is YOU. Edits will happen. Adjustments will and must occur based on your sensations and triggers. Trust yourselves.

Prepare those materials – be prepared to harvest your Blood with a tiny scalpel or lancet, prepare Semen and other fluids via masturbation as this is SELF EFFIGY. All and all this manner of Sorcery puts you back in the driver's seat of your life. I say BACK intentionally, it allows for you to realize, in your hands – that it is all in your control.

DIRECTIONAL SORCERY.....
POLARITIES are important. See the description of the polarities in the beginning of this book.

CONSTRUCTION

Read through this – the directions and the photos follow.

OK – so you should make a twisted paper Effigy. The first one you make will be a simple exercise to show yourself how it feels to make one. You can use this first one if you like, however this is a learning activity. Choose a method. Tell yourself that this is not a moment when you are being criticized about your ability to make dolls. This is a raw muscle you are creating. Build it.

OVERVIEW......

1. Always begin by writing the Parameter of Intention for the Self Effigy. This means, quite simply, deciding what you require from this process.

2. Choose from the 13 categories regarding your purpose. Prepare the materials

3. Make an effigy – twist paper – get it done – and wrap it with thread. The wrapping of the thread is the statement that this is a choice – a thing you are doing – NOT something you have to hold together on your own – not something you must juggle any longer.

4. Rehearse the process in your mind briefly to make sure you are fully prepared.

5. Place the head of the SELF EFFIGY into the polarity that best suits your purpose. Place it down with purpose. You are an adult working on Sorcery alone and have all rights to perform this as you please.

6. After you have placed it in position, take ONE MINUTE OF SILENCE to set your mind into the final actions.

METHODS OF COMPLETION = DISPOSAL......

Completion is the final action regarding the Effigy of the Self. It must be discarded.

COMPLETION MUST BE TRIGGERED

SELF EFFIGIES must be destroyed. They are meant to FINISH an action. Keeping them does not finish the action. Remember the destruction of the EFFIGY is NOT the destruction of the SELF. You are destroying them so that the ACTION is complete. I suggest one of the following

CUTTING THEM INTO PIECES and discarding the pieces

DROWING/soaking them and tearing up the wet paper. You can then discard of it,

BURY the effigy in a place that you do not frequent.

BURN it and dispose of the ash

Any COMBINATIONS of these techniques that trigger completion.

If you are not sure which method of disposal is best for each Effigy, consider a one minute of silence while holding the utilized effigy to explore each of those . ALLOW! ALLOW! ALLOW! your self effigy to gravitate toward one of them.

NOW YOU CAN COMPLETE THE DESTRUCTION. Remember that you are interacting with change. This is not a toy. REMOVE ALL REMAINS FROM YOUR PRESENCE.

THAT IS THE PROCESS. – Now look at the photos before you begin. They will assist you in the construction process...

SELF EFFIGY SEDATION
Three versions of
TWISTED PAPER EFFIGIES-
CONSTRUCTION PHOTOS
SEDATION DATE 4/5/2018
COPYRIGHT
SORCERESS CAGLIASTRO

TWISTED PAPER EFFIGIES

THREE TYPES
KNOT, ONE PIECE & BALL HEAD TWISTED PAPER EFFIGIES

KNOT STEP 1

KNOT STEP 2

KNOT STEP 3

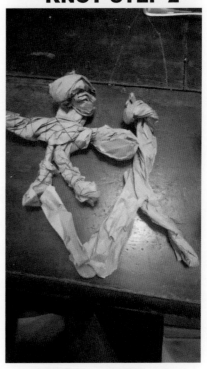

KNOT STEP 4

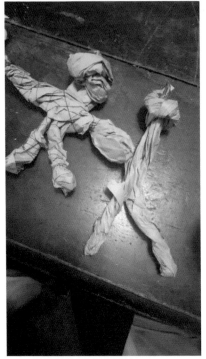

KNOT STEP 5

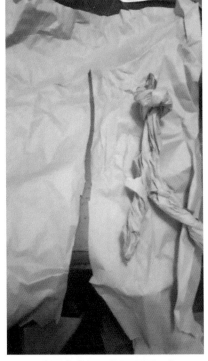

KNOT STEP 6

KNOT STEP 7

KNOT STEP 8

KNOT STEP 9

KNOT STEP 10

KNOT STEP ELEVEN - COMPLETE

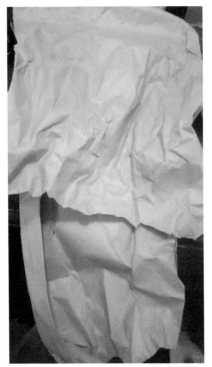

ONE PIECE STEP 1

ONE PIECE STEP 2

ONE PIECE STEP 3

ONE PIECE STEP 4

ONE PIECE STEP 5   ONE PIECE STEP 6

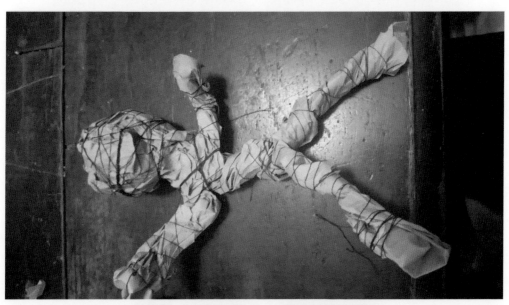

ONE PIECE 7 – FINISHED

BALL HEAD STEP 1

BALL HEAD STEP 2

BALL HEAD STEP 3

BALL HEAD STEP 4

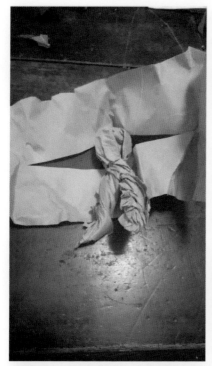

BALL HEAD STEP 5 **BALL HEAD STEP 6**

BALL HEAD STEP 7 **BALL HEAD - FINISHED**

BLANK FOR NOTES

BLANK FOR NOTES

-PART TWO-
EFFIGY USE ON OTHERS

PRINCIPLES, USES, CONSTRUCTION AND PROCESS SPECIFIC TO UTILIZING EFFIGY ON OTHERS

EFFIGY USE ON OTHERS
PRINCIPLES, USE, CONSTRUCTION AND PROCESS SPECIFIC TO UTILIZING EFFIGY ON OTHERS

EFFIGY on OTHERS – Sedation

Please <u>re-read</u> the General Introduction that applies to both sections of this book. It is the OPENING CONTENT to the book.

Original Sedation Date 5/17/18

Regarding utilizing of Effigies on OTHERS.....
DON'T CALL THE MORAL POLICE –
THEY ARE NOT GOING TO RESPOND......

I don't care why you are doing this work on others – I am not the morality police.

USING EFFIGIES ON OTHERS (on line) SORCERY SEDATION (INTERACTIVE CLASS) THURSDAY MAY 17

This experience will teach you to UTILIZE EFFIGIES when working on OTHERS. This process can be used as a stand alone working. or in tandem with THE BOY from the book:

---

29 DEADLY Sigils to Harm, Gain Control or Disarm: Developed with THE BOY, a Daemon from the Hockomock Swamp (AVAILABLE ON AMAZON)

Working with Effigies on Others provides and excellent processes for pulling something to your or pushing something away, revenge, justice and the control of others, of outcome and of the attainment of wealth or pleasure. This is a hot-wired version of justice work. (with Blood Sorcery).

NO PREVIOUS EXPERIENCE REQUIRED. PLEASE REMEMBER TO RE-READ THE INTRODUCTION AT THE BEGINNING OF THE BOOK AS IT APPLIES TO BOTH PARTS OF THIS BOOK.

As the human mind is satisfied by equation.... I suggest the reader/listener begin to think about the equation required to structure the work.

EXAMPLE:

I desire/require_____ + _____ has that skillset + Effigy use = I have that skill set.

THIS WAS A 90 or so minute Sedation. What happened is that participants learned the techniques regarding the building and utilization of the Effigy to be used on others. Participants will be left with this knowledge and the on-going opportunity to decide how to utilize this work toward the attainment of a certain category of manipulations (increased HAVING) in order to secure the desired outcome. I leave it open ended that way on purpose so that you can discover the best results through communication with each Effigy and your requirement of release or attainment.

Effigies to be used on OTHERS are best made of Clay. There will be instructions and directive materials regarding construction as you continue reading.

Images and Photos are provided to assist the participant in the construction and use of these effigies. These Effigies are best used with a small platform I refer to as-

THE LITTLE LABORATORY

A clear image of this is on the cover of this book, and there are other images of it throughout this section.

The photos in this book and will also show up in the recording (should you choose to rent it). As always, everyone who took the Sedation live has gotten at least 48 hour access to this sedation in order to review the work in order to construct Effigies at a comfortable pace.

This opportunity was also useful as, due to the complexity of these types of Effigies, participants could not be making these during the Sedation. Remember these are not art dolls. If you decide to put additional work into them to create a more evolved physical connection with the target, although not necessary, that is fine.

SO on that note – take heed when I mention that - It is important NOT to become attached to Effigies. They are meant to go and do their work and they are NOT connected to you because they are built to impact OTHERS. UNLIKE SELF EFFIGIES, they can remain intact for a period of time, as they are meant to enact long term connections to another person. If you do not desire to keep them around (as some are not placed in second locations) then bury them face down somewhere you are not likely to re-visit. That is **always** the way to get them out of your site line.

These effigies are not DOLLS, they are not ART and they are not voodoo dolls. They cannot be, because this is not voodoo – and with all due respect to voodooists, I say this because that is not my path nor my expertise. What we are doing here tonight is making edits and additions to the interaction between the SELF (or client) and someone ELSE who UPON WHOM THE WORK IS TO BE DONE. This is NOT a sedation about working on yourself per se – it is one about working on the OUTSIDE force/person who is, in some way, interrupting your PLEASURE.

Tonight I am going to introduce you to the following areas of the work:

1.13 categories in which to use of an Effigy on Others
2. METHODS (HOW TO MAKE THEM)
3. RESOLUTIONS/DISPOSALS
4. RELATIONSHIP OF USES TO THE
POLARITIES These instructions will overlap a bit – as that is the nature of process.

THIRTEEN USES OF PROCESS FOR SELF EFFIGIES AS DEFINED BY NUANCES -
EFFIGY ON OTHERS are all to be done on/under
THE LITTLE LABORATOY
(Elevated Glass shown here highlighted)

THE LITTLE LABORATORY (shown above) is a simple glass square (yes it looks like a rectangle in the photo however it is a square) with the Polarities (N,S,E,W) drawn into the corners. The glass is elevated on 4 objects to lift it at least 2 inches off the surface. The area UNDER the glass must be accessible. I used 4 jars here. They happen to be filled with incense by the **great perfumer Darren Alan.** That is just my choice.... The polarities on the glass MUST be placed in their accurate placement.

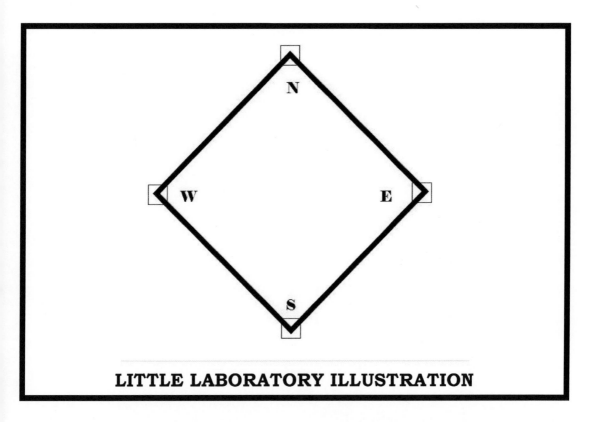

LITTLE LABORATORY ILLUSTRATION

NOTE – WHEN I SAY "YOU" – I AM REFERRING TO "YOU OR A CLIENT OR CHARGE WHO HAS ASKED YOU TO PERFORM THIS WORK". REMEMBER THAT THE <u>BEGINNING</u> POINT MUST BE THE ONE WHO DESIRES THE WORK – AND THE TARGET/LANDING POINT MUST BE THE ONE WHO IS THE SUBJECT OF THE EFFIGY.

READ THROUGH THESE FIRST – THEN CONTINUE ON TO UNDERSTAND THE ELEMENTS/CORE ETC. REQUIRED FOR PROPER CONSTRUCTION

I have included a few photos of the work done on the LITTLE LABORATORY peppered throughout the 13 Categories. **THINK OF THE ILLUSTRATIONS AS EFFIGY SIGILS.**

1.   TO REMOVE AN INDIVIDUAL WHO PHYSICALLY STANDS IN YOUR WAY – REMOVE THEM FROM THE SCENARIO This is focused on removing someone from your physical environment or from another physical environment because they are impacting you in some way which is not pleasurable.

> TECHNIQUE – Place a piece of glass up on 4 pillars so that there is room under it for the effigy. Mark the polarities on the corners of the glass and set them into proper placement. (north facing north). Place the effigy under the glass with its head facing north. Moving it a few degrees per hour, over 6 hours turn it so that the head is facing south. Harvest Blood and put a line of the blood across the center going East-West, & a drop of the Blood (represented by the triangle in the illustration) on the North.
>
> Place in your CORE – Semen or menstrual Blood Place in the EFFIGY – Defining mark, and/or a biological. If you can get hair ripped from the roots. If not then a splinter of glass will do. Mix it into the clay.

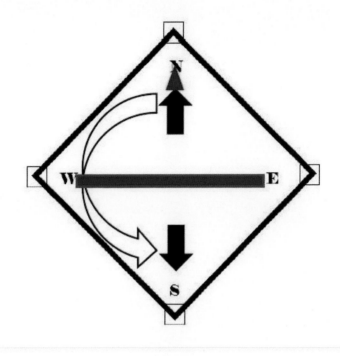

ONE

2. TO REMOVE AN INDIVIDUAL'S INTENT OR THEIR WORK ON/AGAINST YOU. This is the more nuanced method of number one

TECHNIQUE – PLACE effigy face down head south and put a drop of your Blood just behind the effigy, center of the compass, under and over the glass (triangles in illustration)

PLACE IN YOUR CORE – harvested Blood and a piece of fingernail

PLACE IN THE EFFIGY – Defining mark – sexual fluid or a piece of fabric covering the face

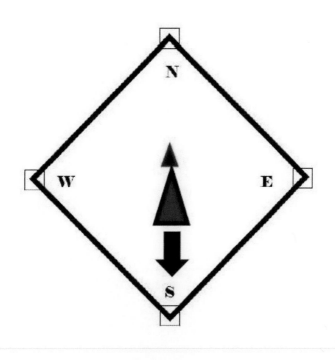

TWO

3. TO FORCE SOMEONE TO CONFESS/TELL THE
   TRUTH just what it says it and a very good option for
   TECHNIQUE – place effigy face up under glass facing
   east with a drop of sexual fluid above the mouth opening.
   PLACE IN YOUR CORE sexual fluid
   PLACE IN THE EFFIGY – Defining mark open the
   mouth and place water in the opening

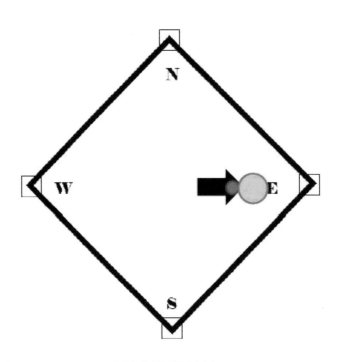

THREE

4. TO CAUSE SOMEONE TO WORK ON YOUR BEHALF. This is useful either directly or by inference. Use when you desire someone to take your side or actually work for you towards attainment of one of your desires – OR to have the work someone does support your side/argument without their knowledge. Example – if someone is doing research or an investigation, create a filter so that all they find is bad evidence on themselves or their principle, and nothing on you.

> TECHNIQUE – place effigy North on top of the glass FACE DOWN NORTH for 24 hours, then under, FACE UP with a drop of Blood & a magnet
> PLACE IN YOUR CORE – Menstrual blood or sexual fluids
> PLACE IN THE EFFIGY – Defining mark any biological of soil from your residence.

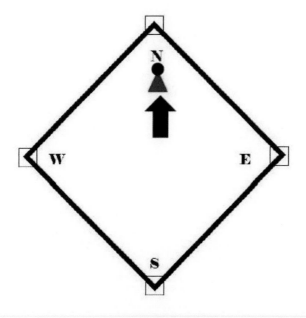

FOUR

5. TO PERFORM INSERTIONS INTO THEIR MINDS
– also good for insertion into dreams. This is used to
either insert and idea or a desire.

TECHNIQUE – use the ball and insertion effigy –
HEAD on top of glass in the center (Human
compass) – core under the glass pointing North. 24
hours later put them together and point them East.
PLACE IN YOUR CORE - blood – drawn if
possible
PLACE IN THE EFFIGY – Defining mark blood
and or hair. Really requires a biological so residuals
from a wiped glass if necessary.

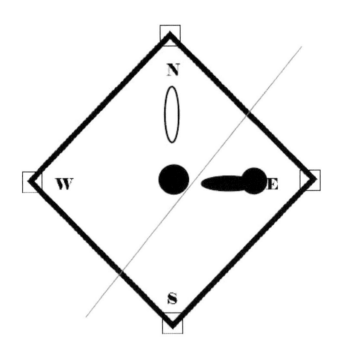

FIVE

6. TO ENACT JUSTICE UPON THEM – two types – one that appears natural to exploit the karma myth, or one that is obviously constructed. This may cause maddening. Use for court cases as well, or to destroy landlords.....

> TECHNIQUE – (reverse of 5) use the ball and insertion effigy – HEAD on top of glass in the center (Human compass) – core under the glass pointing South. 24 hours later put them together and point them South.
>
> PLACE IN YOUR CORE – Blood or menstrual blood, dried first
>
> PLACE IN THE EFFIGY – – Defining mark blood and or hair. Really requires a biological so residuals from a wiped glass if necessary.

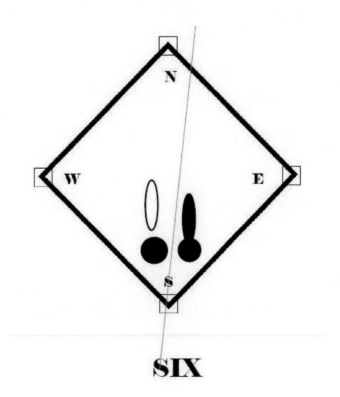

SIX

7. TO UNDO THE EFFECTS THEY HAVE HAD ON YOU. This is a good strategy to remove KNOWN and UNKNOWN trauma. Nuance – trauma that is KNOWN is not necessarily remembered with accuracy – and it does not matter if it is because the feelings and experiences are what matters. So in a way, as all trauma is recalled through a filter of damage – ALL trauma is unknown. This can be assigned to the Self Effigy and removed or worked via this method.

> TECHNIQUE – place South under the glass, face up in water. Spit on glass every 6 hours for 24 hours.
> PLACE IN YOUR CORE – spit and sexual fluids
> PLACE IN THE EFFIGY – Defining mark any biological or residual. Makeup they have used and that sort of this is also usable.

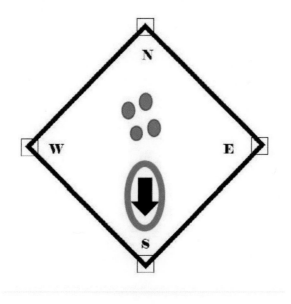

SEVEN

8. TO HEAL THEM. With or without their permission
TECHNIQUE – place 2 magnets NORTH – place
effigy UNDER S, turn every hour for 6
hours/minutes/seconds to NORTH
PLACE IN YOUR CORE – blood or tears
PLACE IN THE EFFIGY – Defining mark
something that represents them to you – biological if
possible also

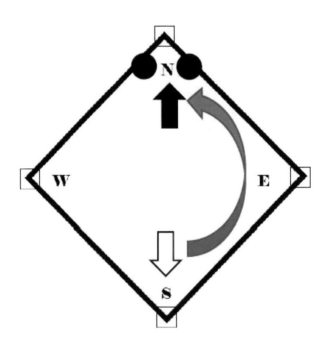

EIGHT

9. TO ERASE THEIR MEMORY OF YOU – to fade you out or to cut you out. Remember you will still have your memory of them, however that memory is often symbiotic so as they totally forget you – your experiences together will fade and you will feel the benefit of that as well

> TECHNIQUE – place the effigy face down under glass, head facing the SOUTH in a drop of your BLOOD & soil from your residence on top of glass in EAST. 24 hours only, then scrape off the blood & bury face down on property NOT YOUR OWN. Place soil from glass **back** onto your property.
>
> PLACE IN YOUR CORE – one hair with follicle attached
>
> PLACE IN THE EFFIGY – Defining mark – soil from your residence

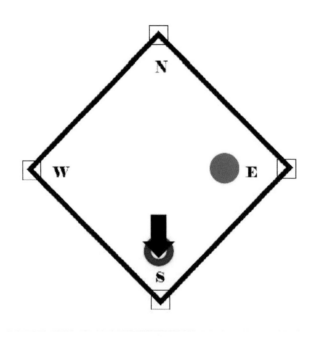

NINE

10.TO ASSIST THEM IN GAINING A SKILL – With or without their permission. Skills are a broad statement. If I baby has a muscular disorder, a skill may be the ability to swallow and therefore feed. A person attempting to get a license in engine repair, learn a language or get a master's degree in complex math etc.

TECHNIQUE - SAME AS 8 EXCEPT CHANGE DIRECTIONS AND ADD ONE MAGNET

place 3 magnets NORTH – place effigy UNDER W, turn every hour for 6 hours to NORTH

PLACE IN YOUR CORE – blood

PLACE IN THE EFFIGY – Defining mark something that represents them to you and the desired skill – biological if possible also

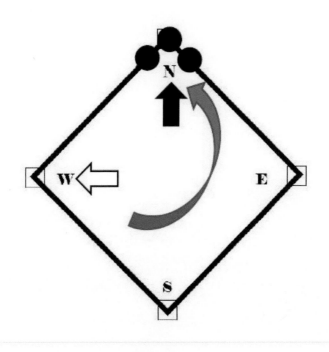

TEN

11.TO ESTABLISH AN ADDRESS IN THEIR CONSCIOUSNESS (MAKE THEM obsess ON YOU) – A living inhabitation of you inside of someone else – the obvious residual is stalking. Beware drama or grief. I did use this for a pop star once and the "target" was "anyone who is obsessed with 'another specific **successful** pop star'. The turnaround was swift. This is useful for sexual obsession also

> TECHNIQUE – they have to be under you facing East–so your Blood in the center position. Several days work best, then place the effigy under your bed.
> PLACE IN YOUR CORE –Blood and sexual fluids
> PLACE IN THE EFFIGY – Defining mark your blood on their "eyes" and iron filings

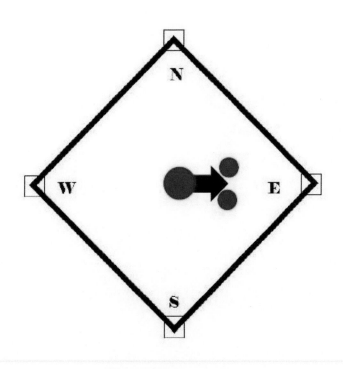

ELEVEN

12. TO TAKE SOMETHING FROM THEM– which means to either take back something you feel belongs to you, take something they have that you desire and require, or take away their wellness and ability to survive. (see 29), TO CAUSE SUICIDE, TO CAUSE DEMENTIA, to cause SUFFERING

TECHNIQUE – place the effigy fully in the SOUTH under the glass. Place your blood all over the south aspect of the glass

PLACE IN YOUR CORE – sexual fluids and Menstrual blood if you can get it.

PLACE IN THE EFFIGY – Defining mark cut into the neck and place soil from THEIR RESIDENCE in the neck. Then wrap it in thread to seal it in.

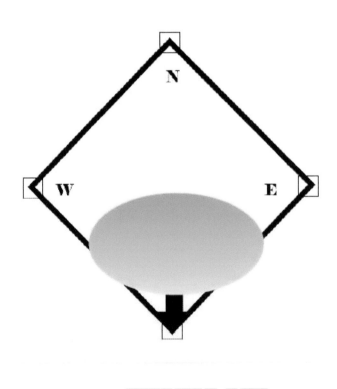

TWELVE

13.TO CAUSE BODYGUARD SYNDROME – use this when you desire to have someone focus their lives on taking care of you. (go ahead – define that....)

> TECHNIQUE – smear your blood under the glass, place a magnet in the NORTH. Place the effigy North with head facing into the smeared blood. Place magnets on all 4 polarities.
>
> PLACE IN YOUR CORE – your hair and blood and sexual fluid
>
> PLACE IN THE EFFIGY – Defining mark one strand of your hair and iron filings

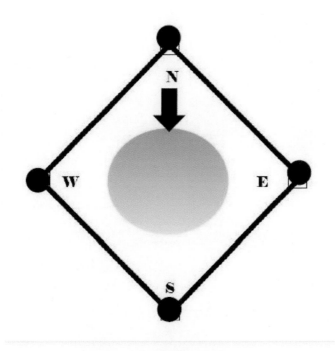

THIRTEEN

METHODS and RESOLUTIONS

CORE OR NO CORE....

Effigies which are to be used to cause another to move or do anything that separates them from the practitioner do not require the core. Effigies that manipulate another to bring something or themselves **toward** the practitioner are best served with the biological core of the practitioner.

BUILDING THE CORE

The preferred material is CLAY that can be baked or air dried. You can also use flour and water however this material often cracks. YOUR BIOLOGICAL. Mixed in and twisted.

Roll a ball of clay in your palms

Flatten it in your palm

Add the intended CORE BIOLOGICALS

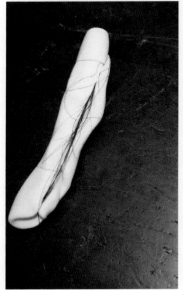

Roll up the core pieces

BUILDING THE EFFIGY WITH CORE – work the effigy around the core. The EFFIGY should be clay and should, where directed, have a core. Here is the list in order of the least to the best functioning EFFIGY ON OTHERS.

1. **LEAST EFFECTIVE** - Twisted paper
2. Twisted paper and their biologicals
3. Twisted paper with your core
4. Twisted paper with your core and their biologicals
5. Clay and no biologicals
6. Clay and biologicals
7. Clay w/w/out biologicals and YOUR core presence.
8. <u>**MOST EFFECTIVE - CLAY WITH YOUR CORE AND THEIR BIOLOGICALS**</u>

These are not dolls. Working with clay or twisted paper puts your own biologicals into the work. Yes, we are of course directing this work towards OTHERS – however **the skin cells from your hands make it clear that you are the MASTER of this act of Sorcery.** They are not there to effect the focus of the effigy toward you. They are there to introduce your strength and DNA into the piece. Your hands manipulate the paper and burn your own heat into it while doing so. The more of these you CREATE, the more you will understand that the twisting and the manipulating of the clay is vital – it is sexual in a way – it is pure physical transference. Working with twisted paper – and, in this case, the preferred medium which is clay, connects the practitioner to the process by ta sensation of a 'physical to mental' path.

This enjoining with the materials is why I prefer these methods to using a doll which already exists. Consider this, if you were just cutting out a paper doll, or using something which already exists, then you would not ENGAGE in quite the same way. **The Engagement is vital.** Thoughts, Ideas and Intentions have weight and the action of involvement with your hands solidifies those intentions.

This is similar to what the religious think a "blessing" is. I have observed the phenomenon of others asking some priest or guru for a 'blessing'. I have watched the moving of the hand to mimic the cross or some similar action. That is simply utilizing an action as a method of visual stimulation to transfer the IDEA that one has RECEIVED something from another who is acting upon some PERCEIVED relationship with a "deity:. When making Effigies, YOU are the perceived 'deity' and the EFFIGY is the servant. This mentioning of the concept of a "blessing" may seem tangential, yet it is not. It goes to the point of demystifying what we are doing here with biologicals and clay. We are taking a THOUGHT, which we have allowed to grow into an IDEA, and we are now acting upon it as a full INTENTION. That puts us in the "deity" seat.

FULLY immerse yourselves when creating Effigies. When fully immersed, distractions cannot withstand the focused hand/mind endeavor. Sounds become less relevant, thoughts outside of the thoughts of the process literally AT HAND fade away. This isn't paper and clay anymore – this is a visceral connection outside of yourself – you are reaching in and touching the ACTUAL TARGET when you are creating these types of effigies.

> The following images will show you the methods used to make both types of clay effigies.

First the construction instructions – then the images to assist you in the construction:

CONSTRUCTION (WITH IMAGES)

First we must start with the core

Roll out the clay (which can be flour and water to simplify but know that it will crack. I use a bake-able clay like Sculpy

1. Collect your biologicals
2. Make a ball from the clay
3. Roll it out
4. Put your biological in it
5. Roll it and twist it.
6. Bake it or let it dry. This is a device for connection. Heating it will not cause you any harm as that is not the intention of the work.
7. Consider making several of these so they are ready when you require them.

Roll a thick column

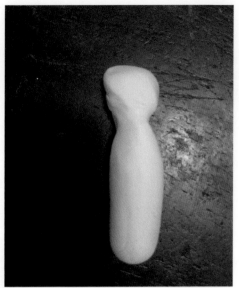

Pinch in a "neck"

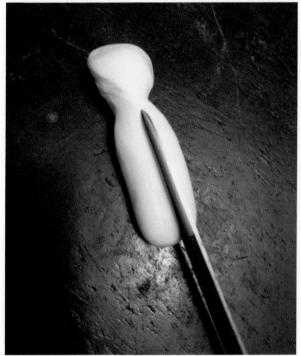

Slice in an opening (don't go all the way through) and open it up.

Push an object into the "neck" to create an opening up into the head.

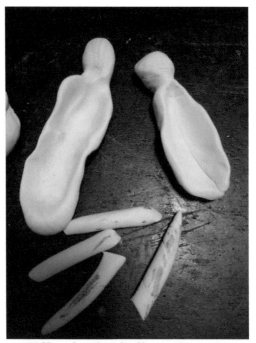

Effigy body shells and cores

Place a core piece into the neck hole.

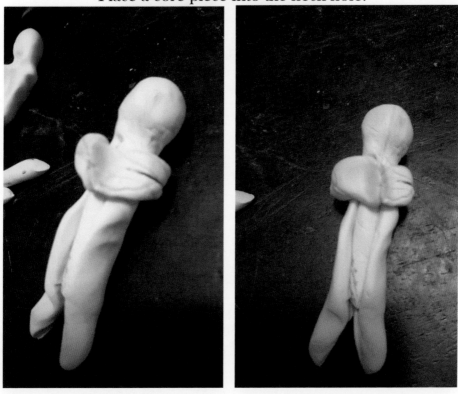

Use another core to wrap as arms and pinch closed.

A SECOND TYPE OF CLAY "OTHERS" EFFIGY

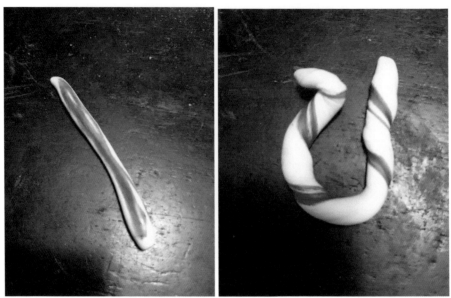

Prepare another piece with Biologicals, twist it as shown

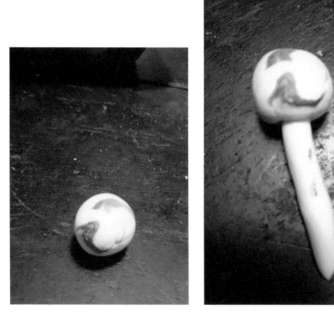

Roll it into a ball and make a hole. A core will be placed inside however it must be separate to start the work so do not /dry them together.

To review the components see:

THE BIOLOGICALS
(see section in the beginning of the book)

+++++++++++++++++**AND**+++++++++++++++++++

DIRECTIONAL SORCERY
(see section at beginning of the book)
A BREAKDOWN OF THE PROCESS

So what do you do with these effigies? Go back through the 13 options and Take a moment to decide......then begin your building process or your **Parameter of Intention** for the Self Effigy.

Remember when working, to place the **head** of the SELF EFFIGY into the polarity that best suits your purpose. Place it down with purpose. You are an adult and have all rights to do this as you please.

METHODS OF DISPOSAL OF EFFIGIES ON OTHERS
It is best to either keep them for the period of time which covers the focused event. If not, then bury them face down on land you are likely to not re-visit.

NOW YOU CAN COMPLETE THE DESTRUCTION OR WAIT UNTIL THIS DATA SHOWS YOU HAVE COMPLETED THE TASK, AND THEN COMPLETE THE DESTRUCTION. Remember that you are interacting with another in this process so data must be gathered from reliable sources. Also – always remember - This is not a toy.

UPON COMPLETION OF THE SORCERY, REMOVE ALL REMAINS FROM YOUR PRESENCE.

THAT IS THE PROCESS.

AFTER you have attempted this work,
If you have questions......
sorceresscagliastro@gmail.com

There will be another Sedation on the subject........

EFFIGY USE regarding **Communication with the Disincarnate**
......soon.....

BLANK FOR NOTES

BLANK FOR NOTES

CAGLIASTRO

Author, Publisher, Teacher, Pleasure Enthusiast, Blood Sorceress, Necromancer, Creator of the Iron Ring Science of Sorcery and the foremost authority on Blood Sorcery, Parent, Explorer, owner of THE FIRM which is a group of elite Sorcerers for hire, Publisher of RESCUING KNOWLEDGE PROJECT (search RESCUING KNOWLEDGE PROJECT on Amazon for newest titles) which reprints esteemed literary works long forgotten for new audiences......

CAGLIASTRO.....gratefully in the hands of 9

+

WWW.NORTHSEATALES.COM
WWW.CAGLIASTROTHEIRONRING.COM

BLANK FOR NOTES

BLANK FOR NOTES

Printed in Great Britain
by Amazon

37138852R00048